Vicky Grosser was born in Victoria, Australia in 1958. She has worked as a community worker for the past 10 years. In 1986 she started to train to teach women of all ages self-defence and has been teaching in London ever since. She also works in a support project for women survivors of sexual assault. She lives in Acton with her partner.

Rani Parmar was born in England in 1967. She trained as a self-defence teacher and uses these techniques in her work with young women. She lives in London with her partner and baby son, and is currently working on an adventure playground in North London.

Gaby Mason was born in 1974 in Manchester, England. She is an active member of her Jewish Youth Club and a student of self-defence. She is now studying at the United World College of the Atlantic, in Wales.

While teaching, Vicky found a lack of self-defence books to recommend to young women, and so asked Rani and Gaby to join her in providing the book they all thought was needed. *Take a Firm Stand* is their first book.

VIRAGO UPSTARTS is a series of books for girls and young women. Upstarts are about love and romance, family and friends, work and school, society and the environment – about new preoccupations – because in the last two decades the lives and expectations of girls have changed a lot. Lively, down-to-the-earth and entertaining, Virago's list is an important new Upstart on the scene.

TAKE A FIRM STAND

The Young Woman's Guide to Self-Defence

Vicky Grosser,
Rani Parmar & Gaby Mason

Published by VIRAGO PRESS LIMITED 1992
20–23 Mandela Street, Camden Town, London NW1 0HQ

*A CIP catalogue record for this book is available from the
British Library*

Printed and bound in Great Britain by Cox & Wyman Ltd

Contents

To young women everywhere
who deserve to be able
to live without the limitations
of fear of violence

PREFACE

To date there has been no book specifically written for young women about the issues of assertiveness and self-defence. The three of us – a young woman still at school, a playworker, and a teacher of self-defence – decided to fill the gap.

Practising self-defence has benefited many young women's lives already. It builds up confidence, and shows you how much stronger you are than you think. It also helps you to be more aware of your surroundings, to reduce the chances of attacks. In addition, practising the physical techniques is a lot of fun, as well as providing you with a range of responses if you should need them.

Contrary to many myths, learning self-defence and assertiveness skills do not make you butch and man-hating. Nor do they make you aggressive or lead you to attack other people. Even if you are small or not very fit, the physical techniques will make a positive difference to your life. Most of all, we hope you will use this book in whatever way you choose, enjoying it for your own purposes.

ACKNOWLEDGEMENTS

Over the eighteen months it took to complete this book, a number of people gave us information, read the chapters one by one, and encouraged us in our writing.

Daphne Tagg – a self-employed editor – answered all our questions, and gave us tips about setting out our proposal to present it to publishers. This eventually led us to our editor at Virago Press, Lennie Goodings. She packed all three of us into her little office, where we celebrated and debated each part of the book with her. Her thoroughness, encouragement and directness were refreshing as each chapter came together. We also want to thank Karen Cooper at Virago, who used her knowledge of martial arts to design the book.

Claudia Silva, from the London Self-defence Project read the chapters on several occasions, using her expertise to help us present the physical techniques in particular. The end product is clear and correct thanks to her generosity. Kaleghl Quinn designed the 'Stand Your Ground' method of self-defence for women many years ago. We are indebted to her for believing that women of all ages can use self-defence skills in every area of their lives. Her approach is effective and practical. It is her teaching which inspired us to write this book especially for young women, and most of the self-defence techniques included in it are her own.

Our friends and loved ones continuously spurred us on. Their honest comments were invaluable. Thanks to Sally Beauchannon and Dinesh Shukla, who cooked our meals and read our drafts, and listened. Also to Stella Mason who generously drove us to meetings with one another. Emma Wade gave us constant encouragement, and read each chapter in great detail: her comments were much appreciated.

We particularly want to thank the young women and men

who made our photographs possible. Hardeep Parmar, who clicked her camera and patiently waited while we practised each position for the techniques, and Ruth Davis for the use of her studio. Then Nicky Parmar, Jassey Parmar, John Wigglesworth, David Mason, Caroline Williams, Azza Brown and John Llanghenheim who modelled the techniques. The young women put all of themselves into each move, and the men were much appreciated for posing as 'attackers' in support of this book for young women.

Lastly, we would like to give thanks to Jacky Fleming for her creative cartoons, to Willow for her drawings of young women used first in Vicky Grosser's logo and now on the cover of this book. Also Dhanwant Rai, Manda Langa, George Theobald and Penny Speirs for the information they provided.

Chapter 1

OUR RIGHT TO DEFEND OURSELVES

I learnt some of it at Self-defence and the rest I made up myself

Why Self-defence?

In recent years there has been increasing concern and publicity about physical and sexual abuse experienced by girls and young women. It is good that this issue is being discussed and that options for resolving it are being explored. At the same time there is a lot of anxiety about the safety of young women – which often places a lot of restrictions on our lives. Fear about travelling on public transport on our own at night, or visiting friends if we have to go through deserted areas, could make us homebound at night.

This fear is understandable – especially with the amount of newspaper and television coverage given to attacks on women. Each week, it seems a young person disappears, or is involved in an attack of some kind. What we don't hear about are the numerous situations in which young women avoid attacks, or stand up for themselves. Parents or carers are encouraged to think constantly about young women's safety, and many are unsure about how to 'protect' these young women. Some adults become over-protective, while others worry about what might happen, yet fail to give young women basic information about the sorts of things to look out for in

1

order to ensure their own safety. This is usually because they don't want to make young women feel too frightened, or because they feel unable to make changes in their own lives.

Because of 'conditioning', girls are often not very confident. They are often told that they can't take care of themselves. For example, we may be told that we can't think as well as our brothers; we may notice that when boys or men are present we aren't listened to when discussions are taking place or when decisions are being made. Although this may not be done consciously, it undermines our confidence in our ability to defend ourselves. We may feel that we wouldn't know what to do. But, as the success stories in the next chapter show, young women have defended, and continue to defend, themselves in a variety of ingenious ways.

What is Self-defence?

There are many reasons why practising self-defence is a useful skill for young women everywhere. As girls we are not usually encouraged to build up and test our physical strength, while boys – on the whole – are left to wrestle with one another. This usually means that they are more at ease with their bodies. Many of us may have memories of being told things like 'girls shouldn't get dirty', and very few of us are encouraged by parents or schools to continue sports beyond a young age unless we are very good at them. This is because our society thinks that girls should learn to be gentle, and care for others in preparation for being wives and mothers; and that we wouldn't be 'proper' women if we continued to mess around and be rough in any way.

Most young women lose confidence in their bodies at an early age, and believe comments such as 'girls are weak'. A lot of us begin to doubt whether we would be able to defend ourselves physically if we needed to. A pretty scary thought. Those of us who have decided to do self-defence have been surprised and relieved to find that we are much stronger than we thought, and can think of really clever ways of defending ourselves using a range of methods we have been taught.

2

Without a knowledge of self-defence we tend to rely on other people – particularly male friends and members of our families – to look after us. Not feeling we can defend ourselves puts limits on our lives: the places we go, the time we spend with friends, and so forth.

Self-defence is not just about defending ourselves physically. It is also about standing up for ourselves when other people say disrespectful or rude things to us. Or when they don't consider our point of view, take us for granted and treat us as insignificant in any way. We all have the right to live our lives the way we want, and to be treated with respect.

Self-defence is about looking after yourself. The aim is to assert yourself, or remove yourself from a violent situation. It is not about revenge, or getting into a fight.

Myths About Learning Self-defence

We have all learned stories about self-defence. Often these include reasons why women shouldn't try to defend themselves. As far as we can see, from our own experiences, and from talking to many young women, these stories are wrong. Here are some of the things you may have heard said about young women doing self-defence:

● girls and young women aren't strong enough to defend themselves;
● if you do try and defend yourself, you'll only get hurt;
● self-defence is silly; young women shouldn't go out alone – they should have someone with them at all times to look after them;
● learning self-defence will make you hate men and want to attack them;
● even if you do learn self-defence, if a really big man attacks you, you won't stand a chance against him;
● if somebody attacks you with a knife or another weapon, everything you learnt will be useless;
● you are too small/fat/thin to defend yourself;

● young women should know their place, and not try and be tough like men;
● if you get attacked by more than one person, you haven't got a chance.

You will probably have heard other things that might have put you off doing a self-defence class.

The more we hear people say things like this, the more we begin to wonder if they might be true. The more we believe these tales, the more we start to restrict our lives and feel that if we are attacked we won't be able to defend ourselves. Kaleghl Quinn, in her book *Stand Your Ground*, calls this the 'attacker within': the voices inside our heads which put us down and in the end make us feel weak and stupid. But many young women have told us how they have defended themselves in a whole variety of situations. These include avoiding attacks or abuse on the streets, or at school or college, by being aware of what might be about to happen and taking action quickly; as well as defending themselves against violence in their homes from members of their families or other people they know.

It would be misleading of us to suggest that young women never get injured while defending themselves. But learning self-defence makes you more equipped to defend yourself without getting hurt in the process.

Why Do People Attack Young Women?

It is not up to you to feel responsible for anybody who attacks you. They are lashing out – because they have been hurt themselves – and you just happen to be there at the time.

There is evidence to suggest that a lot of men who end up in prison because they attacked another person were treated badly when they were young: hit, or neglected, or confused by other people's behaviour. This is a very sad cycle of abuse, but certainly not everyone who is abused gets caught up in this vicious circle.

If you think about when you treated another person badly

in any way at all – which we have all done at some time – you will realise that you were probably feeling desperate, or hurt or confused. Striking out may have felt a relief. Afterwards, however, the old feelings haven't gone away, and knowing that we have hurt another person can make us feel worse about ourselves. Attacking another person is not okay. *No* young woman deserves to be hurt by another person.

Attacks or Mistreatment by Other Young Women
These usually happen because we are set up to compete with each other. This might be over who looks the most attractive (in most people's eyes) or who attracts the young men, or it could be because someone appears 'different' in some way. It may be feelings of jealousy or insecurity that cause an individual or a group of young women to attack another. These attacks usually take the form of gossiping or verbal abuse, or even avoidance so that an individual ends up feeling on her own.

Attacks on Young Women by Men
Most men are taught that females are inferior to males: that they are weaker, can't do practical tasks well, can't look after themselves, and so forth. This means that when these men feel powerless, or angry, or frightened, they easily turn against women. Sometimes their victims are women they know, and sometimes strangers.

Because it's felt that girls and younger women are more innocent and less responsible than older women (this is both sexism and adultism) they end up being more vulnerable to attacks and abuse of certain kinds, particularly sexual abuse.

Our Right To Defend Ourselves

We have all heard people say that everybody has the right to their own space; but what does this actually mean?

Sometimes peoples get too close for comfort, which is an invasion of our physical space – especially if we have not chosen the closeness. An adult may assume it is OK to put an arm around us without asking, or touch us in places we consider to be private. Or we are constantly told what to do, so that in the end we have dfficulty making our own decisions. Some young women have been shouted at a lot, or hit by older brothers or sisters or by their parents. When an adult or older person who is responsible for you abuses you in any way, it is difficult to stand up for yourself, and this can be particularly confusing.

As a result of this sort of experience we can easily end up feeling powerless, which affects all aspects of our life.

Above all, our right to defend ourselves is about valuing ourselves. You are your most precious possession. It is important to look after yourself.

Defending Ourselves: How You'll React

We all have enormous potential, and don't usually live up to it. As we explore a range of techniques we build up our confidence and can start to imagine how we might deal with particular kinds of attack, including those which are our worst fears. If, for example, you are attacked by somebody with a knife, you would react differently, depending on how confident you're feeling at the time. You could

● burst into tears;
● shout loudly in their face;
● kick them in the groin;
● just stand there and talk calmly to the attacker – as a way of gaining time to decide what to do next;
● if you are able to, turn and run.

These are all effective ways to defend yourself, and the options are endless.

No one can say exactly how they would defend themselves in any attack. We all hope when we start learning self-defence that we will be taught foolproof ways to protect ourselves in a range of situations. This is not possible. Every situation is different, and there is a chance that you may get injured.

We always do the best we can to defend ourselves, but other people may not always see it that way. After all, at the time of an attack or abusive experience we have to make decisions

6

instinctively. We deserve to have our judgement of the situation respected afterwards.

> *Amy* (13) answered the front door at home. She was alone. A man she did not know walked straight in and said: 'I'm sorry I'm early, but I'll wait for your father in the front room.' She did not know her father was expecting anyone, so she took him by the sleeve and said, 'No you can't, you'll have to wait outside.' When her father arrived home, she was told off for being rude to a guest. She pointed out that he had taught her not to let strangers into the house.

Trusting Your Judgement

If we do something that endangers our lives while helping someone else in danger, people who are afraid for us often tell us we did the wrong thing. We think that we did the right thing, but it is difficult to feel certain when our instincts are not respected. It is useful to remember this when we listen to our friends' experiences. To encourage and support each other is the best way of making sure we are able to stand up for our rights.

> *Reika* (20), who had done a self-defence course, was on a train in London one evening. She saw two young white men beating up a black man. She was surprised and shocked that nobody was trying to help him. So, in a very schoolteacherly voice, she shouted at them to stop right away. They stopped, and ran off the train at the next station. She waited with the man until the police arrived. She felt really pleased with what she'd done, but her mother felt she shouldn't have spoken up because the men could have turned on her. She was confused because she had always seen her mother help people in difficulty. In fact, her confidence and courageous action were to be praised. She realised her mother was afraid she could have been hurt.

Fears about Learning to Defend Ourselves

When we think about defending ourselves, most of us feel frightened. Because we are scared we avoid thinking about defending ourselves, hoping that if we don't think about it, it won't happen. These feelings are very understandable when we consider that most young women have experienced some kind of attack or abuse in their lives – being 'exposed to' by a man in the street, having a purse snatched, being jostled or whistled at, being bullied by a brother or sister, or getting picked on in school. Some young women have also been sexually abused, either by a stranger or by somebody they know.

Feelings

Once we decide to think about defending ourselves, and learn some of the skills in this book, we feel a range of things. Some of these feelings are exciting – like discovering how easy it is to practise some of the techniques successfully. Other feelings will be less pleasant: realising that sometimes we do need to get angry or feel embarrassed in order to stick up for ourselves. This section is about those feelings.

Feeling Good about Ourselves

Do you find it hard to stand up for yourself when you're feeling a bit low, or tired; or when you have something on your mind which is worrying you?

Feeling good about ourselves is the first stage in defending ourselves. A strong sense of self-worth is where it all starts. We're not often encouraged to praise ourselves, but it's important in getting back a sense of our own value. For example, what do you like about yourself? At first you may find it impossible to think of anything. It's often a help to write down your thoughts: what do you like about your body, your mind, your character? When things are feeling hard and it's difficult to be pleased with yourself, go back to your list.

Often the reason why we find it difficult to like ourselves is because we've been overly criticised in some unhelpful way.

Some of us are told for example, that we have the wrong-shaped nose, or too loud a voice, or that we giggle too much. This sort of disapproval can easily make us feel helpless and bad about ourselves.

Each time we remember another thing we like about ourselves we are getting back our sense of self-worth. We all know that on the days we are feeling pleased with ourselves we are much less likely to let anybody treat us badly. Think of a time you stuck up for yourself and felt happy about it. Did you notice that it made you feel more confident?

Maya (19) told us what happened to her while she was walking along a street near her home. A man was rushing along, and barged into her because the street was crowded and he wanted to get past. She felt annoyed, but then, realising that it was his problem, reacted by laughing. Confused by her response, he said: 'Get out of my way.' Maya laughed again. An elderly woman nearby said, 'Some people are so bad-tempered, aren't they?' Maya was pleased that she hadn't pretended nothing was happening, and that she didn't get into a shouting match to make her point.

Feeling Embarrassed

Have you ever found it difficult to defend yourself because you were worried about ending up looking like an idiot? This is a risk we take when we decide to stand up for our rights, physical or emotional. We think we might make a mistake, or misjudge the situation and that if we shout for help it may not turn out to be as serious as we thought.

There is no harm in acting to prevent something worse happening; shouting for help may even stop something more serious taking place. You may be embarrassed when someone comes to help you and the person who was trying to attack you says he was just going to help you with your bag, but it is far better than leaving yourself at risk. It's important to learn to trust our first instinct.

Feeling Scared

Have you noticed that when you're frightened you tend to hold your breath, and it's difficult to think what to do next? Many people, when telling a story about something frightening that happened to them, say: 'I just froze'. But we can do things to help us unfreeze and decide what action to take next.

Think for a minute about the situations that sometimes frightened you. Some of us start to feel scared on a crowded bus, or when we approach a large group of people in the street. Next time this happens pay attention to your breathing. If you are holding your breath, take some deep breaths. You might also feel a bit shaky, but this is actually useful as it helps let the fear out. You can then ask yourself: 'What are the options for me now?' You might decide to get off the bus and walk for a bit, or cross the road to avoid a large group of people. We can make decisions and take actions when we feel scared. Recognising this is an important part of understanding our power to defend ourselves.

Lai-fong (16) got on a bus to see a friend. It was really crowded, and she couldn't find a place to sit. After a while she started to feel scared. She was sweating, and feeling a bit sick. Her journey was quite long, so she got off the bus and waited until a less crowded one came along. She felt pleased that she didn't arrive at her friend's house feeling shaky, as she wanted to have a good time.

Feeling Angry

Very often any kind of abuse or attack leaves us feeling scared and angry, even if we don't notice this until afterwards. It's a pity that girls are usually told it is bad to express anger, because it is one of the most important feelings when we want to defend ourselves. If, instead of swallowing your anger, you use it to stand up for yourself, it can be very powerful. In most cases it will shock the attacker, and you may well be surprised yourself by how effective it is. Do you remember a time when

10

you got really angry and let somebody know that they weren't treating you well, and how satisfying it felt? No one should abuse us in any way. We have the right to say 'No you don't', and do whatever we feel is best to defend ourselves.

Jasmeed is the middle child of five daughters. Her eldest sister would continually pick on Jasmeed and the others. One evening Jasmeed was going out with a group of friends, and her sister started taunting her, calling her friends tramps. This was the final straw. Jasmeed got really angry and shouted that she was fed up with her criticisms, as her sister didn't seem to have any really close friends so had no right to make comments about hers. Her sister was really surprised, and perhaps realised that it was true. In the end she got upset and cried, and since then she has respected Jasmeed a great deal more.

Using Our Intuition

Intuition is sensing what is going on and making a decision based on that feeling without stopping first to analyse it. In other words, taking action without spending time trying to work out if it's the right thing to do.

The fact is that we all defend ourselves every day: we escape all kinds of possibly dangerous situations, and make judgements about our surroundings which ensure our safety. It might be that we decide to go further up the road to cross it at a safer place; or that we don't accept a lift from someone we don't know.

Being aware of our surroundings and using our intuition is one of the keys to avoiding being attacked. This is explored in Chapter 3.

11

Double Jeopardy

Some groups of young women are vulnerable to attacks – especially out on the streets or in other public places – for more reasons than just being young and female.

Black Young Women

Racism is ignorance, and often includes an unwillingness to learn and appreciate other cultures. It is reinforced by stereotypes in the media. Black women suffer a double jeopardy. Asian women in particular are often portrayed as subservient and physically weak, and Afro-Caribbean women are shown as tough and sexual. They are prone to verbal and physical abuse, quite often for no other reason than the colour of their skin.

Disabled Young Women

In most cultures we are taught at an early age that there is something wrong with anyone who has a physical difference. It may be implied that there is something wrong with their brain, too. People looking for someone to blame can make comments about disabled people, which are abusive and hurtful.

Lesbian Young Women

Society tells us from an early age that our goal should be a heterosexual relationship. However, some young women choose to have loving relationships with other women. Usually this includes a sexual relationship, but not always. A certain degree of physical closeness is tolerated in public, but if young women show that they really care about each other – whether they are lesbians or not – by holding hands or hugging more than briefly, they can get picked on by other people. Attacks may be verbal or physical; both are frightening and isolating.

Other groups of young women are made into scapegoats too. It depends a lot on the make-up of the local community. Think about your school, college or workplace. Who do you notice getting blamed for other people's frustrations? We can all take steps to stop pointless and hurtful targeting taking place. All of us hurt when it happens, because it succesfully divides us and prevents us really getting to know one another.

What You Can Expect from Learning Self-defence

If fear didn't hold us back we would be good at thinking and working out what to do in all kinds of situations. Fear and our conditioning as young women restricts us. The main thing is to listen to and trust yourself. We believe that we do always know what is the right thing to do, even if it doesn't always feel like it at the time. Think about this – and make your own judgement. As we start to practise self-defence we regain our true confidence and learn ways to use our bodies, stand up for ourselves, and be aware of our surroundings – at all times. The long-term aim is to make your life less restricted and more enjoyable.

The aim of this book is to provide you with information, skills and resources so that you can make your own choices about what you do and how you do it, in a way that is aware and that ensures your own safety.

Regardless of your size, shape and physical condition, *you* will be able to use and adapt what we have offered so that it is suitable for what you need in order to lead your life confidently and enjoyably.

After reading this book and trying out some of the techniques you will be better able to think about what makes sense in your life. Think now about how you would like your life to be different and less limited. Use self-defence to combine your mind and body to achieve these goals.

Chapter 2

SUCCESS STORIES

never give up

It is very encouraging to hear about how other young women have defended themselves. It reminds us that we can think and act clearly in all sorts of circumstances.

Ravi (13)

About six months ago I was walking along the street, and a car started driving slowly beside me in the road. The man driving it leaned over and spoke to me through the open window, asking if I wanted a lift. I said 'No', but he wouldn't go away and kept driving along beside me. So I turned round and quickly walked across the road behind his car – and continued walking in the direction I had been going. He couldn't follow me because the traffic was going the opposite way to me on that side, and I saw him drive off. I felt shaky, but pleased with what I'd done.

Rebecca (18)

One evening I was going on the Underground to vist a friend. I walked along a subway under a main road, to save time. I wondered if a man walking behind me was following me, but decided that I must be imagining it. Why would he want to follow me? I thought. Anyway, I walked on past people coming the other way, and started up an escalator to the street. He came up quickly behind me and snatched my bag from under my arm. I turned round and shouted 'Stop!' He looked over his shoulder at me and went down a side entrance to the subway. Something about the look on his face made me decide not to follow him. Later I went back there with my friend and found my bag on the ground with everything in it. It was really scary, because I realised then that it was me rather than my bag that he'd been after. I feel really pleased that I trusted my thinking enough not to follow him when he snatched my bag.

Jasbeer (13)

When I was twelve we used to have my mother's brother's family come and stay with us. My cousin, who is four years older than me, used to pester me when none of the adults could see what he was doing. One day I was hoovering the front room and he came up behind me and put his hand up my skirt. I hit him with the hoover and went and told my parents what he'd done. It felt really embarrassing, but they believed me and spoke to his parents. I think they must have talked with him, because he never touched me again.

Jacqueline (17)

I have always felt that I wouldn't be able to stick up for myself if something horrible happened to me. So I decided to go to a self-defence class which was being held at my local youth club. We had six weeks of being taught to punch and kick, as well as how to get away when someone grabs you, or how to fall to confuse your attacker. We also used our voices to shout loudly and firmly, to stop someone from doing anything to us. I found this part hard to do, but when I was on holiday with my family I was walking in a market-place when a man grabbed my bag and camera. He ran off, and I started running after him. I remembered the voice of my teacher saying, 'Shout loudly to get other people's attention'. So I shouted 'Stop, stop, give me back my bag! Someone help me, that man has my camera.' I was really surprised at how loud my voice was. I didn't seem to be embarrassed like I thought I would be. People in the market turned around and saw what was happening. Some of them joined me in running after the man. Then two men got in a car and drove off after him. At this point I ran out of breath. My family caught up with me, and everybody was talking about it and telling me I did the right thing to shout. I was shaking, and sweating a lot. A few minutes later, the two men came back in their car with my bag and camera. It was an amazing feeling to realise that all this help had happened because I was so noisy. I love telling this story, and I will never be quiet again.

Rita (14)

We used to have a big dog, and we all had to take turns walking him after school. One night I went to walk him by the river on my own. It was quiet, and there was hardly anybody else about. Suddenly, I could hear someone shouting on the opposite riverbank. I thought that they might be in trouble, so I stopped to see what was going on. A man was waving his arms, and dropping up and down – to get my attention. Then I noticed that his penis was out of his trousers, and he was grinning at me. It was really disgusting. I felt tricked into looking at it, by him pretending to need help. Well, I suppose he does need help! Anyway, I just turned around and walked away from the riverbank. It wasn't very frightening, because the river was between us so he couldn't do anything to me. But it still makes me feel sick thinking about it.

Jane (15) and Elspeth (13)

We were out in the big park near our home on our own. It has lots of trees, and there are places which are far away from cars and people. We were walking, and decided to go into a group of trees to have a pee. Elspeth thought she saw somebody behind a tree, looking at us. As she stood, and was pulling her trousers up, a man in his twenties leapt out from a nearby tree and said, 'Pull your trousers down.' Elspeth continued pulling them up and replied, 'No, why?' He told us that he was a police officer, and that girls had been seen taking drugs near that spot. We found this very confusing, and couldn't understand what pulling our trousers down had to do with it. We were now feeling pretty scared and on the defensive. Thinking that Elspeth was being really assertive, I now joined in: 'If you're a policeman, show us your ID, then.' He looked defeated and started to back away, so Elspeth shouted, 'Yeah! Just go away.' Later we told our mother what had happened. She listened, and agreed that the man had come up with a pretty weak story to try and trick us.

Tina (16)

I went to see a film at my local cinema a few weeks ago. While I was in the queue waiting to get my ticket, I saw a young women defend herself. She was really fantastic! A man pushed past her and was really rude when she asked him not to. She shouted back at him. Then he suddenly lifted his fist and went to hit her in the face. She ducked, so he missed, then she punched him in the groin. He doubled over, but was still going towards her so she kicked him hard in the shin. I think she did a couple of other things, but in the end he was lying on the floor. Other people just watched. She had probably done some sort of self-defence, because she seemed to know what she was doing; but maybe she just did what came into her head.

Emily (11) and Caroline (13)

We were walking our dog along a road when a man 'flashed' at us from the other side of the road. Emily decided to set the dog on him: 'Go, Bodger, get him,' she said. The dog started barking really loudly, and the man – now afraid of being noticed by other people, or attacked by the dog – scuttled away.

Sally (14)

I was walking home alone after a tennis lesson, holding my racket. As I wandered along a man started driving a car alongside me. He leered and shouted, asking if I wanted to get in the car with him. I was very embarrassed, and felt vulnerable on my own. I couldn't think of anything to say in return, so tried to ignore him. But he didn't go away, so I stopped walking, hoping that he'd just drive on. At this point he leant right over the passenger seat and stuck his head out of the window. I was scared and angry, which made me take action, and I hit him with the racket and ran away.

Lucy (12)

I was at my older brother's party about a year ago, and I went to see the man who had been showing some slides to everybody. He sat me on his knee and started putting his hand up my skirt. It made me feel sick, but I was also angry – so I punched him on the nose and ran off. His nose was broken. I never realised before how easy it is to break somebody's nose!

Jeanette (16)

I was on a crowded train when I noticed a man smiling at me. I smiled back. Then he moved closer and started feeling my bum with his hand. I frowned at him, and moved away.

Thinking back, I could have done what I was shown in a self-defence class: grabbed his hand and held it up in the air while I said loudly, 'Whose hand is this then?'

Natalie (15)

I live in a city, and when I was about seven my Mum used to let me ride my bike round the block. One day a van drove up and the man inside opened the door and asked me to tell him what I saw. He had undone his trousers and I could see his penis. He kept asking me what it was, and I kept telling him. Then I rode off and told my mother what had happened. She took down the number of his van and reported it to the police.

Mary (21)

I think parents should tell their daughters more about the things that could happen to them. What happened to me when I was fourteen wouldn't have taken place if I had had more information about what boys sometimes do to girls when they're in groups. One day a boy I knew asked me and a friend of mine to meet him in an alleyway near where we lived. We both went there and five boys jumped out and grabbed us. They said they were going to rape us. My friend managed to break away and she ran to get help. They pushed me on to the ground and started taking my clothes off. Then my friend turned up with a couple of adults she'd found and the boys all ran away. I was really angry and felt frightened of groups of boys for a long time; but I was really glad we had been together and that I could trust my friend. Often girls and young women have to help each other like this.

Every time we defend ourselves, we are taking ourselves seriously and valuing ourselves. It is worth stopping to notice when we succeed, to congratulate ourselves.

Think about at least one time when you defended yourself successfully. It could have been by saying something, or

19

running, or using physical force. What do you think you did particularly well? What do you think you might do differently if you were in the same situation again?

Sometimes, when we tell other people about how we defended ourselves, they don't take the time to celebrate what we did. Instead they either tell us about something similar that happened to them or say what they think you should have done – without recognising that you used your own judgement and stood up for yourself successfully. So instead of feeling pleased with ourselves it is easy to end up thinking that we didn't do so well. This may well be one of the reasons why it is hard to think of times when we managed to defend ourselves. Surviving any sort of attack is, we believe, a success, even if we do it clumsily.

Chapter 3

DEFENDING OURSELVES WITHOUT USING PHYSICAL FORCE

How do we defend ourselves without touching our attacker? In fact, this is the most common way in which we stand up for ourselves.

Being Aware of Our Surroundings and Thinking Ahead

This is the first step in self-defence. It is usually possible to be relaxed but also aware of your surroundings, for your own and for others' safety, whether you're inside or outside

When You Are Inside

When we are inside we often feel that we must be safer than when we're outside, and don't take the time to become really familiar with our surroundings. Whether you are in your own home, someone else's, or in a public building, here are a range of things to think about.

Inside Your Own Home It is not always a good idea to let people know if you will be in on your own. If someone comes to the door, ask who is there before opening it, or if possible use a door-chain or peep-hole. It may also be useful to tell a friend or trusted relative how long you will be alone – especially if it is overnight – so that you can call them if you need assistance (or feel frightened), and, if you want, they can check up with you occasionally.

Be security conscious, even if you're tired and would rather just assume (as is true most of the time) that everything will be all right. Check doors and windows, especially when you are on your own. It may be useful to be near a telephone if it helps you feel more secure, but this is not always possible.

Calling for help is not a sign of being a failure. If you're feeling insecure ring a friend: just realising you're not alone can be very reassuring. If you think somebody is trying to break in, or you get a strange phone call, ring the police. They are often called out for what turn out to be 'false alarms'. It is better to phone them than risk dealing with a dangerous situation on your own.

When in a Strange Home Suggestions in the above section are also useful to think about when in someone else's place. The main difference is that it is less familiar than your own home.

If you're baby-sitting, for instance, it is a good idea to find out where the phone is, and all the possible escape routes. It is also useful to know who to call if you should need assistance: for example, a friendly neighbour. You may want to give the phone number of where you are to a family member or friend.

When in a Public Building

Looking around you in any new place is important, and this applies equally to public buildings: colleges, schools, sports halls, libraries, and so on. During the day it may well feel very different, especially if there are lots of people around, than at night-time. Knowing the escape routes and exits, as well as who to call on for assistance at different times, makes good sense.

In any building, if you have strange feelings about someone – even if they are in a position of responsibility (such as a

22

caretaker or teacher) – do trust these feelings and either get out, or find somebody safer to be with.

> *Linda* (16) was in the reference section of a public library early one morning, revising for her exams. It was a quiet side room, which had only one member of staff at a desk, when she wasn't busy doing something else. Linda noticed a man watching her from a nearby table. He appeared to be reading a newspaper, but obviously wasn't really concentrating on it. After a little while he started wandering around the room, looking over his shoulder in a suspicious manner. At this point the librarian wasn't in sight, and only one other person sat at the far end of the room. Linda felt annoyed about being disturbed, and decided that she didn't want to study in this uncomfortable atmosphere. She moved to the main library tables, and continued with her work.

When You Are Outside
Many of us get from one place to another by foot, or on a bike and often this can leave us more exposed to possible attack than when we are in cars or on public transport.

Local journeys are easy to take for granted. During the daytime you may feel safe walking or riding across places like your local park or common, or open areas such as car parks, shopping precincts, alleys and quiet roads. It is important to be aware of the surroundings and notice your feelings about the area. Stay alert, so that you are listening and looking around in a relaxed way. Walking positively, so that you appear confident, is an important deterrent to attacks. If it's dark or raining hard, or there aren't many other people around, you should stop and reconsider your route. It is also important to remember that attacks are just as likely to happen to young women during the daytime as at night. It isn't stupid to take a longer way round because you feel wary. Trust your feelings and judgement. If you think you are being followed, stay as calm as possible, and get to a well-lit place or somewhere with are other people, or choose a route, if possible, with houses along the way.

How You Look: Your Posture

If you feel confident and good about yourself it shows in the way you move. When you walk down a street looking scared and ungrounded you will seem frightened to other people. A potential attacker is more likely to choose you if you look depressed and vulnerable. We all have times when we feel sad, tired or unwell, and this can show in the way we move or in the expression on our face.

> *Kofi* (17) was walking along the road deep in thought. A man stopped her, put his face right near hers, and said: 'Cheer up love, it's not the end of the world.' She turned to him and responded, 'Look, I was just thinking. Don't interrupt me.' Obviously he had interpreted her expression in a very different way.

We are not suggesting you should walk around pretending to be happy all the time. But do be aware of how other people are reacting to your body language. Look around you when you're next on the street. Or at your friends. Do they look pleased with themselves, or scared, or depressed? Our feelings do affect the way we look. Notice what happens to you when you feel happy or sad.

It is possible to 'fake' what we feel. If you feel ill, or have had a bad day at school or college, try to notice your surroundings and look confident.

Getting Home Safely

It is a good idea to think ahead about how you are going to get home, even if you will be with friends. They won't always be going home at the same time, or to the same district.

Are the clothes you are planning to wear the best to have on when you travel home? You might want to take something to change into, for example shoes you can run in if necessary, and clothing which is loose enough not to restrict your movements.

At night-time, wherever possible, walk in streets that are well lit, even if this makes your journey longer. If you go along a certain route frequently, try to be aware of shops, or other places where you could get assistance if you should need it.

Avoid being out alone if you have had something to drink, or anything else has happened that might affect your behaviour and make you less alert. For example if you've had an argument with a friend and feel upset it may make you less aware of your surroundings. Taking any kind of drugs will affect your awareness and judgement.

Take precautions, such as walking in the opposite direction to the traffic to avoid getting dragged into a car. Even if you have a long walk ahead of you, don't accept a lift with a stranger or anyone you feel uncomfortable with. Saying 'No' *is* OK; you're not obliged to make them feel happy.

If you get followed, yelling 'Fire!' is often a better way of getting attention than shouting 'Help!'

It is worth always having some small change with you in case you need to make a phone call.

Sit near the driver on buses, so that if you feel under threat you can ask for assistance. Avoid empty compartments on trains: this may mean moving to another carriage half-way through your journey, even if it feels embarrassing.

Ask people who look reliable (especially women) to walk with you if you have to walk along a quiet road after travelling on a bus or train. If possible, arrange for someone to pick you up to avoid walking on your own. If it feels embarrassing, you can always ask them to wait in the car just round the corner.

Jamila (16) *and Kalpana* (15) were returning home by foot, after visiting their sister and her family who lived nearby. As they were talking, Jamila thought that she noticed several young men following them. She told Kalpana, who wasn't so sure, and said, 'Oh, you do fancy yourself.' But they quickened their pace just in case, and took a couple of sudden turnings as they knew the area well. By now the three men had caught up with them, and so they stopped by a garden gate. They were starting to feel really afraid. One of the men singled Jamila out, and started stroking her hair while standing very close. It was very sexually intimidating.

Kalpana became enraged, and began shouting at them really abusively. Without saying anything else, she moved inside a garden gate and rang on a doorbell, pulling Jamila behind her and shouting all the time at the men.

Various thoughts went through their heads: what if there was nobody in? What if a weird man answered the door and they had to escape again? The young men were hanging around by the entrance, watching them. Kalpana and Jamila started discussing men they knew, as though they would be answering the door in a minute. A man did come to the door, and looked slightly confused at first. Then he caught on, and responded to their request for help. He told them to come in while he called the police. Jamila asked him to call their brother-in-law instead, who would come and pick them up. When he arrived the young men were still hanging around, but walked away pretty quickly. Afterwards Kalpana and Jamila realised that they had taken a risk by ringing on a stranger's doorbell, but they had done exactly the right thing.

Often when young women have been attacked, they say afterwards that they got signs that something was going to happen long before it actually did. But they didn't trust their own judgement, and as a result ended up dealing with more than they would have had to if they had listened to their intuition.

Ultimately it is up to you: you have to use your own judgement and make your own choices in each situation. But you don't have to do it all alone. For example, you can ask someone to listen while you decide what to do before going out. Rather than making you feel more afraid, planning should make you more positive about where you are and what you are doing. In the end this means that you can enjoy yourself more.

If You Are Being Bullied

Most of us have been bullied at some time in our lives. It might have been by a brother or sister, by someone at school or college, by friends who suddenly seem to turn against you, or by an adult such as a teacher, adult relative or youth worker. Sometimes young women are so badly bullied that it affects every area of their lives.

Terri is thirteen years old. One of us was involved wth supporting her through a really bad patch of being bullied at school.

She had always been popular, and got into conflict with another young woman, called Amanda. Amanda, feeling that her own popularity was under threat, set about turning other young women against Terri, by stopping them from talking to her. Terri asked her teacher for support. After a few weeks the teacher couldn't understand why the bullying still continued, decided that Terri must have done something wrong, and stopped supporting her. Terri felt totally isolated, and stopped going to school. She told the workers at her local adventure playground about the bullying, and they also tried to help. In the end Terri changed schools, because she wanted a fresh start. At first she told a few people what had happened at her last school, to reduce the chances of being isolated and to prevent anything similar happening again.

Terri got very frightened by the bullying, and called on other people for support. She didn't give up when one adult stopped helping her, and in the end she made a decision. Although this disrupted her life in many ways, it gave her the opportunity to renew her confidence and get her life moving again. She tried not to stay isolated. At no time did she use physical contact to defend herself, and she continued – with the support of others – to talk about the difficulties she had experienced with the other young women.

Running Away

If things are beginning to look dangerous we can run away. This is an excellent way of defending ourselves.

Sara (14) was coming back from an ice-skating class when it was dark, although not very late. She noticed a man staring at her when she was getting off the bus. He got off too, and she felt a sinking feeling. Was he following her, or wasn't he? She had about a five-minute walk to her home, part of it up a short alley. She walked fast, but noticed she was getting more and more scared. When she looked behind, the man was still following. At this point she decided: who cares if I look weird to other people, I'm going to run. So she headed off fast up the alleyway, and around the corner of the next road into her own street. Only then did she stop and wonder if he was really following her.

Who knows?, she thought – but I didn't have to hang around and find out. She didn't tell any of her family about the incident, because she thought they would probably think she was crazy. This is very common. You probably have memories of keeping things to yourself, because you thought people wouldn't understand what you were feeling, and be supportive without judging or worrying about you.

Staying Still

Often, when we feel under threat, there is a strong urge to 'do something fast' to 'save' ourselves. In some situations, acting quickly is a good solution. But, staying calm – at least on the outside, even if you are feeling very scared inside – is a really smart way of standing up for yourself.

The following incident happened in the school playground. The young woman, Penny, who told us about it was thirteen at the time.

I was standing in a queue, waiting to go into the dining-room for dinner. I had been waiting for a long time, and a group of young men in front of me were starting to get really wound up. They were teasing each other, and other people waiting. I have very long hair, which I wear in a plait. Suddenly one of them grabbed the end of it and started saying it was time to cut my plait off. I was embarrassed, but only a little afraid, until one of his friends got out a pair of scissors and started snipping them in front of my face. By now, lots of people were watching in fascination – some of them laughing, and others sort of holding their breath. At first I felt angry, and humiliated. Then I thought: they won't really do anything to my hair; just stay calm and wait. It felt dreadful – the suspense – but in the end one of the group who used to be in the same class as me told the others to leave me alone. After another snip or two, they started teasing somebody else.

Who knows if the way this young woman reacted saved her hair! It was successful in her eyes, and although other people might have done differently, it was the best she could think of – and pretty brave. No doubt you have been in situations where you noticed yourself thinking that just staying still and saying nothing was the best way to respond.

Acting 'Crazy'

Deciding to act in a socially unexpected way – acting weird – is another option for self-defence.

In a class Vicky taught at a youth club, she asked each of the young women to invent a way of putting their attacker off without touching them. They came up with a fantastic selection. Here are some of them:

● fainting in front of the attacker, just as he is about to grab you. Either he will walk away, or get so confused that you can roll over suddenly and run away. It gives you time to think, but being immobile on the ground does make you vulnerable;

● suddenly developing a 'tic' – an uncontrollable twitch in your face which makes you look out of control. Again this is off-putting, and gives you time to think;

● picking your nose, really thoroughly! Most people find this disgusting, and are likely to leave anyone who does it well alone.

● pretending to have a seizure. If you have ever seen another person have a fit you'll know that others tend to get frightened and don't know what to do. This is irrational, as obviously such seizures are not dangerous to other people. However, the young woman who tried this out in the class found that the person 'attacking' her became confused and didn't know how to respond;

● pretending that you're going to be sick. Many people hate this, and feel revolted. So it can be very effective!

Using Your Voice

There are a number of ways in which using your voice can prevent an attack from developing further.

Shouting at the attacker, in a firm voice. Using short and sharp words is more effective than long sentences. For example, you can shout 'No!' loudly in their ear. It is very disorientating to be shouted at, and it makes the point that you don't want to be messed around with. (Remember to take a good, deep breath first, or it won't work so well.)

Repeating a question or a statement is also a good way of taking control. You might ask, 'Why do you want me to do that?' Don't get side-tracked, just keep asking, even if you get an answer. Or, 'I will not be bullied by you, so go away.' It is difficult for the 'attacker' to continue to do/say what they had in mind if you are firm in this way.

Summoning help, by using your voice. Calling 'Help!' is not, in the view of many self-defence teachers, the best way of getting others to come to your assistance. Shouting 'Fire!' is supposed to be more effective: people tend to run to see where the fire is, out of fascination. The main thing is not to continue shouting long sentences. Keeping this up eventually gets exhausting. Keep them short and loud, and take good breaths in between.

Lastly, talking to someone who is threatening you is also known to work well. If you can keep calm enough to ask what they want, or what the matter is, it will help them see that you are still in charge. Most attacks are about people trying to get attention or to humiliate the person they're attacking in order to feel powerful. They will tend to choose people who seem weaker than themselves. By talking to them you can show that you won't be put in this role. It also stops you from freezing up and gives you time to make decisions about what to do next.

How have you noticed other people using their voices to stick up for themselves: on the streets, at home, in films, at work/school/college? Did you notice how it affected the 'attacker', and any other people who might have been around? Are there some things that worked better than others? Try these voice methods out with a friend. Notice how it feels to be on the receiving end. Which do you find most effective, in a range of different situations? Being loud, in particular, is not usually encouraged in young women. As a result, some of us have ended up with quiet and unassertive voices. Trying out these methods is a fantastic way of getting our voices back. (You can always start by shouting into a pillow if it feels too embarrassing to let rip.)

Being Fluid

This technique involves moving quickly and sharply, in lots of different directions. It is a clever, and ingenious method of self-defence, which requires reasonable fitness. You need quite a lot of space for it.

Get a friend to try and catch you, in a wide, open space. Keep twisting and turning – even if they get hold of you briefly – so that you keep in control. Roll over if you feel confortable on the floor/ground, and change the speed to further confuse them. Then swap over, so that you can see what it's like.

Pretty good, isn't it!

Inventing Your Own Techniques

You have probably gathered that the list of things you can do to defend yourself without using physical contact is endless. What we have included in this chapter is a good selection of what we have heard of young women using, and what we think makes good sense. Carry on inventing your own ideas, and notice that it is a real pleasure to expand ways of defending yourself – without using physical force.

Chapter 4   PREPARING TO DEFEND OURSELVES PHYSICALLY

This chapter and Chapter 5 cover the physical techniques of self-defence. For most of them you don't need to be very fit. When you read about these techniques and look at the photographs you may feel that you don't actually fancy trying them out. Many may seem strange at first. However, we do encourage you to practise them together with a friend. This way, they will become familiar, so that if you need them in the future you will know what you are doing.

WARMING UP

Before practising the physical techniques, it is worth taking the time to prepare your mind and body. Rushing into them makes it harder to concentrate, and you are more likely to pull muscles and injure yourself.

These exercises aim to warm up all the parts of your body, including parts you may not use often - depending on what sorts of exercise or sports you do. Many of them are based on the Stand Your Ground method of self-defence, which is designed by Kaleghl Quinn. If you know other exercises that use the same parts of the body, do them instead or as well.

Remember to breathe while you warm up. It is easy to find yourself holding your breath as you do the exercises.

Starting with your head and neck

Stand in a relaxed but upright position. Take a few good, deep breaths, then slowly tilt your head sideways, then over to the other side. Now tilt it forwards - taking your chin towards your chest - and then back to the centre. Next, rotate it in a semicircle all the way from one side to the front, and then to the other side, and back again gently. Do this a few times slowly, in each direction. Again take a breath - to relax - and then a really big breath in as you lift your shoulders up to your ears. Then let the breath out loudly as your shoulders go back down. Repeat this a couple of times.

Now warm up those legs

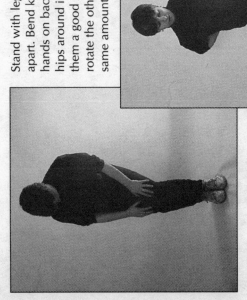

Stand with legs hip width apart. Bend knees a little. Put hands on back of hips. Swing hips around in a circle, to give them a good stretch. Then rotate the other way, for the same amount of time.

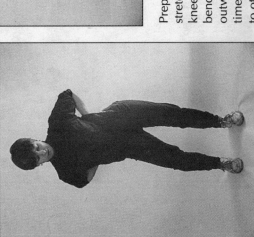

Prepare legs for kicking. Turn to right, and stretch right leg out to side. Bend toes towards knee. Bend other leg slightly. Clasp hands and bend over outstretched leg. Scoop down and outwards to stretch back of leg, for about eight times. Don't go too low, take it in stages. Change to other side.

Stand with legs close together: knees and ankles touching. Bend knees and place hands on thighs. Keep rest of body still, while rotating knees in a circle in one direction: about ten times. Then change the direction for the same amount of time.

Moving up to your arms

Spread legs wide apart. With chin down, stretch linked hands above head. Then - as you breathe out - swing arms down over one leg, and back to centre. Repeat stretch, then second side. Stretch again, and swing down between legs. Repeat exercise, slowly, twice.

Put one foot in front, and one behind body at an angle. Breathe, and swing arm - on same side as front leg - backwards in a circle slowly. (This stretches sides of the body and lungs.) Change legs, and use other arm.

Speedy exercises
Now we change the pace a bit!

Find a reasonable-sized room, or space outside. Start by walking in a circle slowly. After a bit, change the direction. Gradually increase the speed, until it turns into a gentle jog. Again change the direction.

Now as you run, lift your arms and rotate them forwards slowly. Then swing them backwards.

Again change the direction. Then bend your arms, and take the elbows down to touch the opposite knee as the leg comes up. Breathe normally.

Now gradually slow down to a walk. Rest and relax !

Exploring your strength
Stop a minute before you go on, especially if this is the first time you have done any sort of self-defence or martial art.

How strong do you think you are? Are you feeling weak, or not very confident and wondering if you will be able to do the physical techniques?

Strength is a big issue for young women. Most of us are told from an early age that girls are not very strong, or that we are too small/ too fat/ too uncoordinated to defend ourselves. After a while, it is easy to believe these messages. We are not saying that you are as strong as a big, male, bodybuilder, but the reality of it is that you are always stronger than you think you are. It is usually difficult to remember this, and the following exercise is a fun way to test it out.

Press-ups
You don't have to do fifty press-ups to feel the benefits. Press-ups will quickly make your arms and shoulders stronger, especially if you're able to do them every day or two. They also make you look more confident and more relaxed.

Lie on the floor with forehead on ground.

Put hands, with fingers spread, by shoulders.

Turn toes under. As you breathe in, lift body smoothly to straight position.

Breathe out, go down, and relax.

The Unbendable Arm (based on Kaleghl Quinn's Resilient Arm Exercise)

You'll need a partner to do this exercise.

Part 1

Clench fist, and rest back of wrist on partner's shoulder.
Partner uses both hands on inside of elbow to bend arm.
Try second arm.

It is not a competition. The aim is to help each other to explore your strength. So don't go on straining until your back aches.

How did it feel? Was your body relaxed or tense? Did you breathe normally, or hold your breath? Did you grit your teeth?

Part 2

The aim is to use your strength in a relaxed way, so you don't run out of energy and get exhausted. Take plenty of time.

Imagine your arm is the branch of a tree or something strong and flexible as you again place back of wrist, with open hand, on your friend's shoulder.

Stand with feet well apart, and knees bent. Imagine they're rooted like a tree.

Think: 'She won't bend my arm', and breathe evenly as she presses down.

Repeat with other arm.

You probably noticed that it was much easier this time: less effort and more relaxed. Let your friend have a go, and notice the difference for her. This relaxed but confident kind of strength is what we are aiming for all the time and it makes doing self-defence a lot more enjoyable.

Part 1

Part 2

38

Getting grounded

This is not about lying on the floor to defend yourself! All the techniques in the next chapter involve you being well balanced and standing firmly on your feet.

Try out this exercise to notice the difference between having your body weight firmly rooted like a tree or being wobbly on your feet. Again you'll need a partner.

Part 2

Part 1

Relax, and let a friend pick you up off the ground from behind.
Notice how easy it is when you're not 'grounded'.

Part 2

This time, bend knees and concentrate on staying attached to the ground.
Breathe out evenly as your friend tries to lift you. See how much harder it is. If an 'attacker' was trying to drag you it would be hard for them to go any distance while you were using your energy in this way. However light you are, grounding is the key to doing the techniques in the next chapter effectively.

A fun way to try it out is to stand on a moving train or bus and see how long you can stay upright, not holding on to anything!
Now move on to do the techniques in Chapter 5.

Part 1

CHAPTER 5   USING PHYSICAL CONTACT TO DEFEND OURSELVES

This chapter includes a range of techniques and effective methods for responding to a variety of possible attacks that involve physical contact, either because you have been grabbed by an attacker, or because you choose to prevent (or end) an attack by defending yourself with physical force.

The emphasis is on surprising the attacker: doing something unexpected to take charge of the situation. It is not about getting into a fight. Self-defence is about doing just what is necessary to ensure your own safety.

These techniques are all very effective, but don't feel that you have to stick to them. Experiment and develop your own ideas. After all, this is how these methods were invented.

However, there are certain precautions to take because you can injure yourself. We do our best to point these things out as we go through the different techniques. The general rule is to look before you aim at a target.

HOW WILL LEARNING THESE DIFFERENT TECHNIQUES HELP ME?

There are many advantages to learning these techniques:

- They make us more at ease with using our minds and bodies together, which is necessary if we are to use the techniques effectively.
- For many of us, learning these techniques gives us an opportunity to discover our real strength. We find that we are stronger than we'd thought.

Some of these techniques are based on martial arts such as karate or judo, while others have been developed as day-to-day practical methods of self-defence. Many are based on the Stand Your Ground techniques devised by Kaleghl Quinn.

We want to stress that there is no one ideal way of responding to a particular attack. While we indicate that some of the techniques may be effective responses to certain types of attack, ultimately it is up to each young woman to decide how and when to use them. Every attack is different in some way. It is for this reason that *we strongly encourage you to practise the techniques until you feel familiar with them. This is what makes the difference in the long run.*

- We sharpen our ability to think clearly and invent ways of reacting to all types of unwanted physical contact.
- We find out how to prevent ourselves getting hurt.
- It gives us the opportunity to notice how we feel when we experience different kinds of physical contact.

41

HOW DO YOU FEEL ABOUT BEING TOUCHED?

How you feel when somebody touches you on different parts of your body and then how you respond is a big issue in self-defence. A lot depends on how you feel about your own body, and what kinds of positive and negative contact you have had in the past. Think for a bit about the parts of your body that you don't mind being touched by people you know, and by those you don't. In addition, each culture has different 'norms' about which parts it is ok to let others touch.

FEARS ABOUT HURTING OTHERS, OR GETTING HURT

These fears will affect how you feel about using the techniques on an attacker. For instance, how would you feel about poking another person in the eyes?

The thought of injuring somebody in this way may be very off-putting, but if you were attacked by someone who was about to get very violent this could be a very good defensive reaction. It is unlikely that you will ever need to use this response, but it is a part of learning self-defence to explore these issues.

On the other hand, getting hurt yourself may be your main concern. This is always a risk. It would be irresponsible of us to pretend that young women never get hurt. Learning self-defence does, however, reduce the chances of getting injured badly. Bruises are inevitable if you practise the techniques.

It is very useful to become familiar with the 'blocking' techniques at the end of the chapter.

They reduce the chances of somebody punching you, for instance. We encourage you to be firm with one another when learning them with a friend so that you create as realistic a situation as possible. If you are concerned about whether you would be able to defend yourself against a large adult man, then ask a father, uncle, older brother or some other man to help you practise.

Finally, it is worth remembering that in learning these techniques with a friend you will feel much safer than in a real attack. So your feelings – fear and anger for example – will be different and less intense, when you are practising.

STARTING WITH THE ARMS

Repeating the 'Unbendable Arm Technique' in Chapter 4 will help you to remember to ground yourself, concentrate and breathe evenly when you are using these techniques.

Punching

Start by practising into the air, then make yourself a punch-pad, either by rolling up blankets or by using pillows which can be held by somebody else, or placed in the back of a heavy chair or on a bed. This way you can practise punching at different heights and angles.

Remove any rings. Make a fist, with thumb outside to avoid spraining/bruising it. Start with fist on hip. Step forward, breathe out and hit right through target, keeping wrist straight to avoid injury. Pull fist back after contact in preparation for next move.

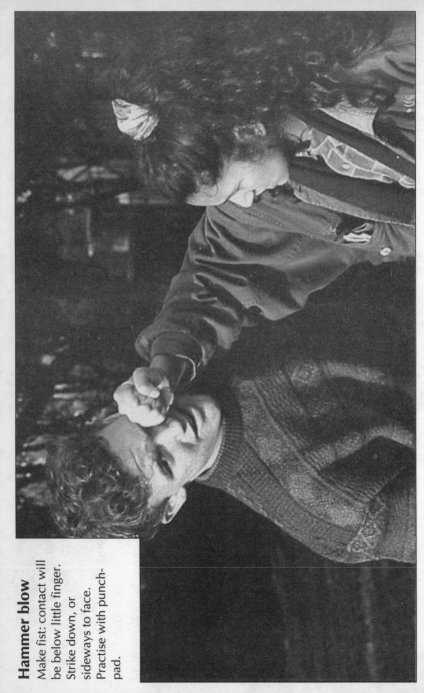

Hammer blow
Make fist: contact will be below little finger. Strike down, or sideways to face. Practise with punch-pad.

44

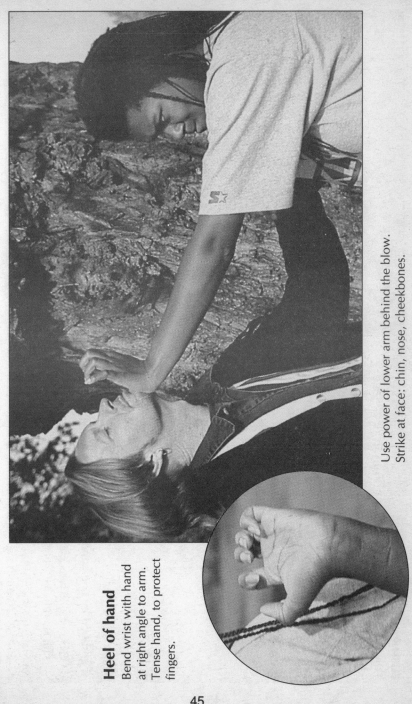

Use power of lower arm behind the blow.
Strike at face: chin, nose, cheekbones.

Heel of hand
Bend wrist with hand at right angle to arm. Tense hand, to protect fingers.

45

Arm grabs

Having an arm grabbed is a common first stage in attacks. Remember to stay well grounded, and breathe evenly to reduce the amount of energy you have to use. The aim is to free yourself at the place of least resistance between the thumb and fingers of the attacker's hand. Here are some useful methods:

If grabbed by one hand on your arm

(a) Grab base of attacker's little finger. Pull sharply back and out at angle.

(b) Make fist with hand of grabbed arm. Firmly flip arm in circle from shoulder to break hold.

If grabbed by two hands on one arm

Make a fist with hand of grabbed arm.
Cover with other hand to put all body behind action.
Step firmly towards attacker into their 'space', to put them off-balance.
Then flick arm downwards to break the hold.

It is important, once you have released your arm, to follow through with some other action: for instance punching, kicking, running, using your voice.

47

Scratching

Clawing or scratching, especially to the face, is very painful. Scratching other parts of the body will depend on what the attacker is wearing.

Imagine your hand is a claw of a wild animal. Strike forward and downwards, sharply. Clawing at an angle on the face does more damage.

MOVING ON TO THE LEGS AND FEET

Legs, like arms, vary in strength, mainly depending on how we use them, especially what kind of exercise we get. If you walk a lot, ride a bike, swim or dance, for instance, you will probably feel pretty confident about using your legs. Here we aim to give you a range of ways of defending yourself with your legs and feet.

Kicks

Where you kick an attacker will be influenced by your height. We show you how to aim at shins and knees.

Forward kick

To avoid breaking toes, kick with them turned back, striking with ball of foot.

Stand firmly on supporting leg.
Lift knee of kicking leg, then strike forward with foot.
Breathe out as you keep spine straight to stay balanced.
Aim below knee for best effect.
Snap foot back to be prepared for next kick.
Practise with something to aim at.

It is also possible to kick backwards (although harder to aim well) with the ball of the foot, or the heel.

Side kicks

Bend knee, then strike sideways as you breathe out.

Hit target with outer edge of foot.

It is also possible to use this type of kick when you are on the ground, to keep an attacker away.

Aim for the kneecap or just below.

With kicks, the most important thing is not to lose your balance: either by kicking too high, or by leaving your leg too long in the air so that an attacker can get hold of it and tip you over backwards. So don't aim higher than you are confident of kicking with force, and get your foot down to the ground straight away.

For fun, try doing a lot of kicks with one leg without putting the foot on the ground in between. It will build up your stamina.

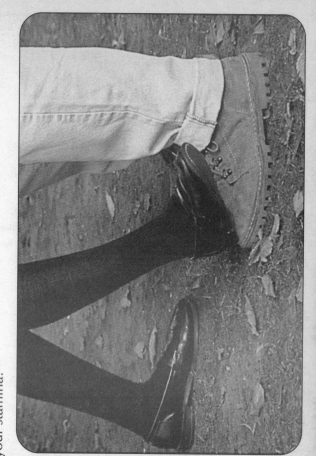

Stamping

Hard-heeled shoes, or high heels are most effective.
Stamp down very hard, putting all your weight behind it.
This is less successful if the attacker is wearing very hard shoes or boots.

HOW AND WHERE TO STRIKE IF NECESSARY

As we learn the techniques we wonder about what parts of an 'attacker's' body to aim for with the different methods. Some parts of our bodies have more nerve endings near the surface than others, so they hurt more if you strike them. For instance the outside top of the arm isn't very sensitive, so isn't such a good place to punch somebody when you are defending yourself. The diagram here is based on the information given by Kaleghl Quinn in her book, *Stand Your Ground*.

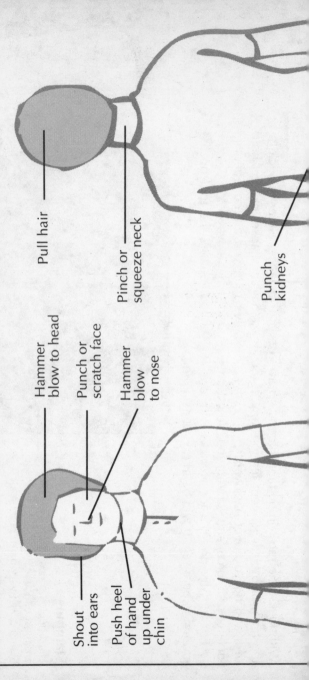

Pull hair

Hammer
blow to head

Punch or
scratch face

Hammer
blow
to nose

Pinch or
squeeze neck

Punch
kidneys

Shout
into ears

Push heel
of hand
up under
chin

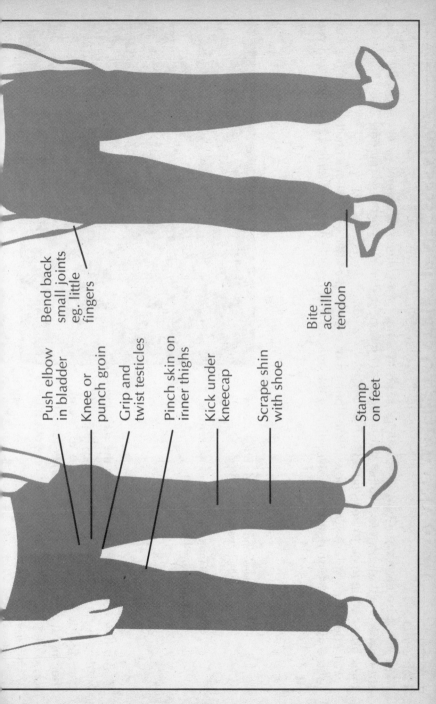

Bend back
small joints
eg. little
fingers

Push elbow
in bladder

Knee or
punch groin

Grip and
twist testicles

Pinch skin on
inner thighs

Kick under
kneecap

Scrape shin
with shoe

Bite
achilles
tendon

Stamp
on feet

Hair pulls

Most young women have had their hair grabbed at school, in college, at home, or occasionally in the street which makes them feel vulnerable. Obviously it depends on the length of your hair, but it is hard to think about what to do to free yourself when it hurts so much.

You could kick, or use your elbow in the stomach or groin of the attacker. Here is another effective way to free yourself which doesn't involve injuring the attacker, but does leave them feeling confused and you in control.

Bend knees, and twist whole body around. The pain will make them let go.

Put your hand on top of the attacker's, to trap in and reduce the pain.

If your hair is long, you can reduce the pain by holding it above the attacker's grasp. Then you can decide what technique to use to break their hold: for instance, stamp on their foot. Try lots of different angles and places on your hair to see what works best for you.

54

Biting

Not everyone wants to sink their teeth into other people. However, it is very painful to be bitten hard. As with scratching, where you bite will depend on what parts of an attacker's body are available and what clothes they are wearing. You can turn your head sharply as you bite, to cause more pain.

Although the chances are small, biting which draws blood can put the biter at risk of contracting the HIV / AIDS virus.

Strangleholds

Hand chokes

Being choked is a particularly frightening kind of attack. Unlike most other holds, where you can wait a bit to respond, it is important to act fairly quickly before you run out of air and faint.

If you have a sensitive neck let yourself giggle until it feels less ticklish.

Get a friend to put their hands around your neck from behind.
Tilt down chin, to protect throat and keep breathing.
Grab base of their little fingers and pull up and back firmly.
Follow through with a punch or elbow to stomach, or whatever is appropriate.

From the front the method is basically the same. If you have difficulty getting hold of the little finger, try another one. Use your voice too, to show confidence and anger.

Arm chokes

As with hand chokes, this stranglehold needs fairly quick action. Keep breathing and thinking about your next move.

Get a friend to grab you around the throat with their arm.

First sink chin into crook of arm. Use hands to grasp arm to create space to breathe, as you drop your weight down. Elbow them in the groin/ stomach or stamp hard on their foot.

Even if you get lifted off the ground, you can still kick backwards.

FALLING SAFELY AND FLEXIBLY

We hear people say things like, 'be careful, don't fall over', but falling is in fact a great way to defend ourselves. You will probably get some bruises, but falling is a good way of confusing the attacker, as long as you get up quickly to avoid being kicked.

You need to protect your head, face, knees, elbows, wrists and back.

Use a bed, or judo/ sports mat if you have one available. Just roll about and get familiar with protecting your arms and face, as well as the other vulnerable parts of your body. Keep breathing normally, and stand up to shake your body to loosen it up when you notice it getting tense. The main tip is to keep moving, so that you reduce the impact of hitting the ground if you do fall when defending yourself, either on purpose or by mistake. This will make you more confident about looking after yourself, and braver about using a broader range of the techniques.

Escaping a bear hug

If an attacker comes up behind you and hugs you, with your arms inside the hug, you may well feel very helpless. Ask somebody to grab you in this way, and experiment. It takes a bit of courage, but try this technique:

Tuck chin in.
Drop down suddenly
like a dead weight.

Push bottom backwards
against attacker's legs to push
them off-balance.

Keep moving, roll over and stand up quickly.
The attacker is left very bewildered.

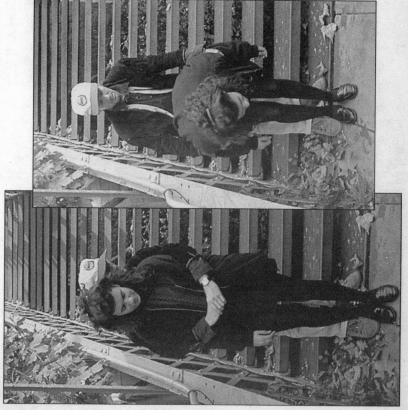

DEFENDING YOURSELF WHEN PINNED ON THE GROUND

Have you ever had anybody push you to the ground and then sit on you, pinning your arms down? It is a pretty frightening experience, and you feel very helpless. Take a breath, and notice you're still alive! Relax a little.

The element of surprise is very important with this technique.
Bring knees up, feet firmly placed on the ground.
Growl to release energy and twist body, using hips to throw the attacker off to side.

60

Follow through with a knee to the groin, or a punch.

Try using the same method of flicking your hips to push an attacker away when you are pinned against a wall.

Remember if one method doesn't work, don't give up. Try another technique to free yourself. The surprise element disappears when you practise these techniques with a friend. They know what you are going to do. In a real situation you can surprise an attacker.

THROWS

The thought of throwing someone, especially if they are bigger and seem stronger than you, may appear very unrealistic.

The aim of this section is to demonstrate that however small or lightweight you are, thowing another person is not nearly as hard as it may seem. However, we do want to stress that *it takes a good deal of practice to throw somebody who is larger and a lot heavier than yourself.* The reason why we have included this technique is to give you the chance to try it out; to discover the range of options open to you.

Be sure to practise throwing somebody on a low and soft surface: sports mats or mattresses, at the very least. Do the throws very slowly at first, to avoid injury.

When throwing someone, you need to position yourself below their centre of balance, usually their hips, to tip them off-balance. We have included only one type of throw for you to learn; it is unrealistic to try to demonstrate others in a book. If you find this one inspiring, try and get yourself along to a self-defence class or martial arts course.

Hip throw

Get a friend to put an arm around your neck from behind.
Clasp this arm above the elbow with both hands.
Step firmly to that same side.
Bend at the waist as you pull down on arm towards opposite foot.

They will tip over your hip, and land on the ground on their back.
Do this very gently with your friend. A fast fall will wind someone badly. *It is very important to be well grounded when you throw someone else, or you risk falling with them..*

BLOCKING AN ATTACKER'S PUNCHES

One part of self-defence is being prepared to defend youself against an attacker's punches.

You can step to the side of an approaching blow, or turn and run. But knowing that you can deflect or push the punching arm of an attacker away from its route to your body, is very reassuring.

First of all you need to be very firm on your feet, with knees bent to improve grounding. Resist the urge to lean back, which you will want to do if you're afraid. Stay grounded. If you move forward, do it with all of your body, and step in after blocking to return a punch, or other blow. If you are carrying a bag or some other item you might choose to drop it to defend yourself, but it could be very useful to hold this up to block an attacker's blows or attempts to grab you. Think of the ways you could use it.

Raise arms at right angle.
Place hands with fingers spread, to see through, in front of face.
As attacker punches, use the lower arm (it is much stronger than a hand or wrist) to block. Don't push out, but keep your head and face covered at all times.

WEAPONS IN ATTACKS

The prospect of being attacked with a knife or a gun is very frightening. Police figures suggest that it is much more common for men to attack other men with weapons. However, mugging (holding someone up and threatening or injuring them to get their money, jewellery or other valuable items) with a weapon does happen to women. On occasion more violent attacks, including rape, are carried out with a weapon.

Here we explore issues about being attacked by someone with a weapon, as well as self-defence with the use of weapons.

Being attacked with a weapon

What we can demonstrate in a book about dealing with weapon attacks is limited of course, but we can show some basic principles. If you want to learn how to defend yourself against knife attacks, for instance, we suggest you go to a class where you will be taught these skills well.

Sue (18) was attacked by a man with a knife. He pushed her against a wall in the street and said that he was going to rape her.
She was very scared, but looked him in the eye and said 'No you're not'.
He was so surprised he stopped holding the knife in front of her.
Then he walked away.

Using her voice was very successful in this young woman's case. It takes courage, but getting the attacker to see you as a person, rather than an object to assault, is one approach. It does involve breathing evenly and staying outwardly pretty calm, which gives you time to think, and decide what action to take next.

Get a friend to hold a toy knife in front of you, or across your throat, or in your back. Notice how scary it feels, and see what phrases you can think of to get her talking while you think about what to do.

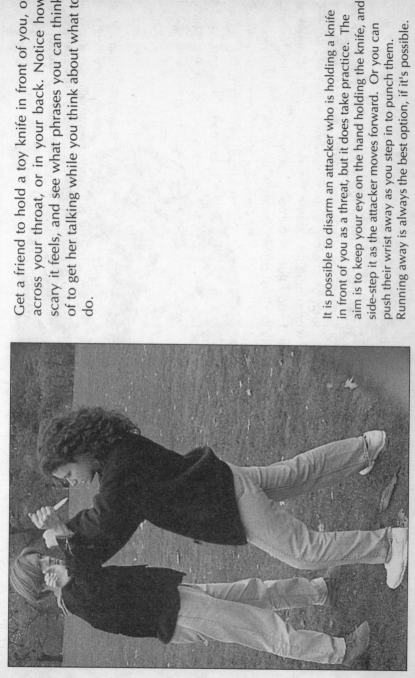

It is possible to disarm an attacker who is holding a knife in front of you as a threat, but it does take practice. The aim is to keep your eye on the hand holding the knife, and side-step it as the attacker moves forward. Or you can push their wrist away as you step in to punch them. Running away is always the best option, if it's possible.

Using weapons in self-defence

The law is different in different countries. (You can ask a local advice agency, or the police about your rights.)

Don't carry a hammer if you're not a carpenter, as you can be charged with carrying an offensive weapon. Young women have used objects such as chairs, lamps or umbrellas in their houses, schools or workplaces to defend themselves with. It is likely, though, that if you injure somebody badly you will later have to explain why you used the 'weapon' you did. This law is to prevent people from defending themselves without good reason. In the end, as in any attack, we each have to judge it and make the best decision we can.

Generally it is all right to use anything which is available as a part of your everyday studies (rulers, pens, books) or work to defend yourself with.

It is possible to buy alarms to frighten an attacker. These are operated either by battery or by gas cylinder. It may make you feel, and therefore look, more confident to carry one. However, you need to have it in your hand, not in a bag or pocket, so that it is readily available.

USING THESE TECHNIQUES FOR SELF-DEFENCE

A range of self-defence techniques has been worked out as practical and effective aids for women of all ages to use. We have done our best to give you information about those we think are most useful to young women. But as you try them out we hope that you will invent others which relate to your own physical fitness and expectations about how you would react in a variety of different possible attacks. Learning self-defence can be a lot of fun. Building up a whole new set of skills doesn't have to be frightening. It will enable you to feel confident about looking after yourself well.

Chapter 6

WHAT HAPPENS IF YOU GET ATTACKED?

How do you feel?

Young women experience a number of things, and are faced with a range of choices about what to do, after any type of attack. What you choose will depend a lot on the nature of the assault, which may be a verbal attack (including bullying), a physical assault (including rape), or an attack of a sexual nature (including incest).

It is commonly believed that there is only one correct way to respond to any particular kind of attack. For example, it is OK to cry for a while after being rejected by a friend, but if you wake in the night in a sweat and can't face going out the next day, many people might think this is an 'over-reaction'. In our view, each young woman has to deal with any experience which is distressing to her in her own way. Each of us is different, and will react differently in the way we deal with the same kind of situation.

What we aim to do in this chapter is to cover the range of feelings young women experience after a variety of incidents, as well as how they get support from others in order to recover. We all deserve assistance to help us get over the effects of any kind of attack: to make the choices and take charge of our lives again in whatever way we think is appropriate.

Getting Support to Recover from an Attack

However serious, or not, you feel an attack, assault or bullying has been, we recommend that you find somebody as soon as possible to tell about it. It could be a friend, or a relative, a teacher, doctor or youth worker. Or you might choose to go to the police, or some support agency. This prevents you from having to deal with any consequences of the incident on your own.

> *Katrina* (16) was pressurised to have more sexual contact than she wanted with a boyfriend at a party. Afterwards she felt confused and angry. She spoke with her aunt, who was very sympathetic. She listened to Katrina and helped her decide how she would deal with a similar situation in the future.

You could also use this support to think about how you tell others if you wanted to – for example family members – about the incident if it's something you think they would find difficult to hear.

All types of abuse – physical, sexual and emotional – have a profound effect on our lives. They can happen to any young woman, regardless of class, background or culture. It is a common myth that working-class young women experience worse abuse from family members than others. This is not true.

What you do after such an attack is your choice. No one has the right to make you feel guilty or stupid for deciding either to report, or not to report, the attack. If you choose to report it, here are some useful pieces of information:

● it may be necessary, due to physical injuries, to go to a hospital as soon as possible. It is worth knowing that if you have been sexually assaulted or raped the hospital staff are legally bound to inform the police. For this reason it may be a good idea, where possible, to have someone else go with you to the hospital;

● if you decide to report an incident to the police, take a trusted adult or friend with you, for support. The police should be happy for you to do this;

● it is important not to wash or change your clothes if you think they will provide evidence for the police;

● try and remember everything about your attacker(s). You may want to write down their colour, height, build, hair and eye colour, clothing and any distinguishing marks. Also note their accent, and rough age;

If you don't want to report the incident to the police, it is still important to get support to recover from the effects of the attack. Use the list in Chapter 8. If they are not directly able to help you, these agencies can refer you to someone else who can.

Any sort of assault or attack on a young woman is illegal, regardless of whether the woman knows the 'attacker' or not. It can be particularly traumatic to be assaulted by somebody you know, and trust. Many young women are hit by relatives or carers, and a significant number are sexually abused.

If you are in a sexual relationship which is making you afraid, guilty or unhappy, with someone in your family or household, (whether they are directly related to you or not) then you are experiencing incest. The abuse may have been going on for some time, and the abuser may have been bribing you or threatening you to prevent you telling anyone else. This is because they know that it is not acceptable behaviour to use a young woman in this way. You may feel as though it would be a betrayal to tell on this person, or you may think that you would not be believed. The important thing to know is that you do not have to put up with this abuse. There are now a number of very good agencies which provide support in exactly this kind of situation (details of these are in Chapter 8).

Other People's Reactions to Attacks on Us

There are many false and misleading ideas about physical, emotional or sexual attacks – and in turn these affect the way people respond to others who have been assaulted. Young women, understandably, are afraid of being disbelieved or blamed after an attack. People may say unhelpful things like, 'Why didn't you scream?', or 'What were you wearing?', or 'You shouldn't have been alone in that place.'

Other people's feelings can leave us feeling guilty and responsible for what happened to us. When you tell others about an attack, they quite often don't know what support to give you. If they are parents, or adults who are responsible for you (for example teachers, youth workers, other relatives) they too may feel guilty, which in turn leads you to feel responsible for their pain. In the end, you are left dealing with the consequences of the attack in isolation.

Greta (14) had her bag snatched from under her arm when walking along her high street. Her parents' response was: 'You should have a bag with a proper strap you can put over your shoulder.' She didn't need to be criticised then, but listened to until she worked out how she might have dealt with the situation differently. It is OK to make mistakes. She deserved support.

A common reason for adults failing to give good support is that they think that young women and girls are irresponsible, or because they are worried about their safety. For instance, adults often question how young women look, thinking that wearing make-up could lead up to them being assaulted.

Ideally, it is more helpful if those close to you understand and respect your need to do whatever it takes for you to regain control of your life – both the emotional and the physical aspects – after an attack.

Regardless of what happens to you, you always did the best you could at that time, and should never be blamed for the attacker's actions. If the people around us can't offer all the support we need after an attack, there are a number of good agencies which have experienced and skilled staff to assist young women. Details of these are in Chapter 8.

Feelings

It is very common to feel any combination of the following feelings after an attack:

Numbness	Shock	Fear
Guilt	Shame	Depression
Confusion	Anger	Helplessness
Mistrust	Sadness	Grief

Some people say that you can expect to feel these emotions in a certain order, but it is not always that simple. One day you may walk around feeling numb, and thinking it just isn't possible that this has happened to you. The next minute this can switch to humiliation or shame, and then you may find yourself reacting angrily in an inappropriate situation and realise that this feeling is linked with the incident. You may not recognise what the feelings are at the time as the range of emotions you experience can leave you feeling very confused.

There is no 'correct' way of feeling after an attack – it depends on the individual. It is easy to think, on top of everything else, that we should be feeling something or other now, which just side-tracks us from recovering. There is also no 'perfect' time-span to respond to your feelings: it depends on what else is going on in our lives at the time, and on what sort of support we get from other people.

Here are things to think about or notice in relation to some of the common feelings, after any kind of attack.

Anger
After an attack you may find great feelings of rage coming to the surface. How dare someone assault me? What can I do to get my own back? A general loathing of all people vaguely reminding you of the attacker is common, too.

For example: *Gurjeet* (17) was insulted by a group of white men in their twenties, while on a train one evening. She is still very wary of groups of white men in this age group, and feels she would like to get her own back at them in some way.

Other people around you may also be angry for (example your parents), which may make it feel as if there isn't any space for your own fury. As mentioned earlier, you may find yourself reacting inappropriately in a different situation: finding mild irritations turning into outbursts of fury at people who had nothing to do with the event.

Above all, don't blame yourself for being angry. It is quite appropriate to be indignant about any sort of attack; it is a part of standing up for yourself and maintaining a sense of your own worth.

Shock

It is also very common to experience a kind of trauma after an attack: a sense of disbelief that it took place. Some people act as though nothing has happened for a while, before something triggers another feeling to rise to the surface. You will probably have heard this being called 'delayed reaction'. It can be quite disturbing to witness in another person, and if it happens to you other people around you may either start telling you to let the feelings out, or pretend that nothing has really happened. Neither approach is very helpful: we need people prepared to listen as we deal with the feelings, and to remind us that they want to hear about it, stage by stage, without judging or blaming us.

In extreme cases, especially when we have had a very traumatic experience and there has been no one to support us in the way we need, we can completely block out an incident. Many people experience later in life a sudden recall of something that happened to them years ago. If they hadn't blocked it out they might well not have been able to function on a day-to-day basis. It would simply have been too much to cope with.

Grief

After any sort of attack or assault many people feel a sense of loss or bereavement. The person who you were before has been violated in some way, and it can feel as though you've lost a bit of yourself. Sometimes young women who have been bullied, for example, feel that they've lost their confidence and this affects every area of their lives, including friendships. Regardless of the level of the assault, most individuals feel sad in some way.

Fear

Fear operates at a variety of different levels. It is frightening to remember what happened, in case you should ever be in a similar situation again. If the experience was not a major one (according to your own judgement, not someone else's), it will probably not be too scary to talk or think about it after a while. However, if it was very frightening at the time, the fear will stay until you have had a chance to deal with it. You may, for example, find yourself shaking or sweating, or even giggling 'hysterically' – quite natural ways to recover from anything scary – when you are in a vaguely similar situation again. For instance if the attack was on a bus you might feel pretty 'nervous' about travelling on buses for a while. This is completely 'normal', too. The level of fear will often be linked to whether you were attacked by someone you knew or not, and the degree you trusted them if they were a friend or a relative.

You may also find the fear creeping up on you when you are in safe surroundings where you know you can trust the people around you.

For instance, *Karen* (20) was abused by somebody in her family as a child. She always felt tense and on edge whenever she was at home – even years after her abuser had stopped living there. It was only after she left home and was living with a good friend that she noticed she'd wake up sweating in the night after having scary dreams. Now there was someone who was nothing to do with the situation at all supporting her – and at last all the feelings, including the terror, could get to the surface. It was a great relief.

Fear can take many forms. Some people find they suddenly can't move, or speak: being 'frozen with terror'. It is realistic to expect that you will need support to do some things which you did alone before an attack; whether it's going to school, travelling on public transport, being in the house after dark, answering the phone, shopping, or whatever. The aim is to take things stage by stage until you are back to being yourself again.

Mistrust
Early on in our lives, each of us expects that other people will treat us with respect and that we can completely trust them. Then, as time goes by, we all experience some kind of mistreatment by others. Any type of assault or abuse is a shock, and adds another layer of hurt and mistrust in people generally. It is also usual to find that a certain type of person – for example a white man with a beard and glasses – reminds us of someone who mistreated us in some way. As a result we may find on first meeting him that it is difficult to decide to trust him. As time goes by it is easier to think of this man as a separate person, and if you like him the mistrust will go away.

Guilt
Most people feel that they were in some way responsible for getting attacked. 'Did I do something to make the attack happen?' A common example is the clothing we wear. Society

stereotypes young women as irresponsible and naive. If, for instance, we are sexually harassed it can easily feel as though it was our fault.

> *Danielle* (13) felt that wearing a short skirt may have led men on a building site to whistle at her. She raised this in a class Vicky was teaching. All the other young women agreed that she should be able to wear whatever she chose, and that it wasn't her fault that the men reacted in the way that they did.

Rather than concentrating on how we could have stopped an attack, people should congratulate us on having done the best we could to handle it, regardless of how serious it was. Criticism is not helpful; it is unsupportive. Given time, we will be able to review the incident for ourselves and make our own judgements about how we might handle a similar situation in the future.

Many young women say that parents or other relatives make them feel guilty. Usually this is because the relatives feel responsible for your having been attacked. Obviously this isn't very rational, but given the way in which society expects parents to be more than perfect at all times, it isn't a surprising reaction.

It is, though, our right to expect total respect from everybody around us after an attack.

Depression
People become depressed to varying degrees: from finding it hard to get up in the morning, to sitting silently and eating very little, to sleeping all the time and having no energy. An extreme form of depression can lead to feelings of wanting to kill yourself.

It is frightening to be depressed, and part of it usually includes not knowing what to do. If you notice yourself starting to become depressed after an attack, get some assistance from a reliable person. They will be able – especially if they are skilled – to help you talk things through and deal with the feelings which have got buried in the hopelessness. Then you will begin to feel more in charge of your life. This could be a teacher, youth worker, parent or other relative, or a counseller from a support organisation for young people. Above all, it is not your fault if you get depressed.

In conclusion we believe that – although it can take some time – every young woman can completely recover from any kind of attack. Whether it is a single incident or a repeated assault over a long period of time, once we have good support and have dealt with all the feelings we need to, we can get ourselves back, fully. It is up to each of us to take the journey to complete recovery in our own way. In the process you will have learnt a lot about yourself and gained more self-respect and confidence. You may go on to help others who have had similar experiences.

Chapter 7

TAKING SELF-DEFENCE A STEP FURTHER

you mean like THIS

Having read this book, and explored some or all of the techniques in Chapters 4 and 5, you may want to take practising self-defence a step further.

There are a number of options for expanding your knowledge, or getting together with other young women to practise the techniques and learn others. It will depend a lot on where you live: in a city there are more likely to be classes in self-defence for young women, or you might want to do a particular martial art such as karate, judo or aikido. Youth clubs often have this kind of information, or you could telephone your local council or town hall and ask for their information service.

If you don't live in a city or large town it may be harder to find local classes or groups to join. If there isn't anything available, you could ask your school or college to run a class.

Setting up a Self-defence Class in Your School or College

Here is a basic plan for setting up a class yourself.

● Ask friends, and young women in your class, if they would be interested in a self-defence class.

● Inform groups such as the Parent Teacher Association that the young women want a class.

● Approach a teacher of self-defence. You can find names of teachers by, for example, contacting a youth centre, or women's project.

● Next work out costings, and other details such as the kind of space needed, the maximum number of young women in a class, and whether mats are available.

● Now is the time to approach women PE teachers to ask if they can help with use of the gym, and some of the money for the teacher's fee.

● If your school is not willing to put self-defence on the curriculum, the PTA doesn't want to give any money towards the costs, and the PE staff aren't able to either, there is another option.

● You will have to ask the young women attending the class to pay for it. Work out the amount each person would have to pay each week to cover the costs. Charge for the classes in advance of the course, which will also be a good incentive to those coming to attend all of the classes.

● Publicity is important. Put details about the class (time, place and cost) in the school or college newspaper, if you have one. Also give details to the PE staff to pass on to the young women they teach. Put posters up, too.

● Ask the self-defence teacher to support you by coming into the school to meet form teachers as the class is being set up. This will get more support, and hopefully encourage more young women to attend.

So, if you want to set up a class, find adults/teachers to support you. Show them this book, and any newspaper articles or other examples of how self-defence has been useful to young women, and perhaps get your friends to put their names on a list of support for a class.

Finally, if these options don't work or aren't practical, get a group of friends together. The chances are that between you

you can teach each other techniques that any of you know. You can also spend some time thinking about what self-defence means to you and possibly plan a campaign to get better facilities in your area,

Chapter 8

INFORMATION ABOUT THE LAW, AND USEFUL CONTACTS

The Law

How the law affects you will depend on which country you live in, where the attack or assault took place, and what kind of incident it was.

This section covers the general law relating to self-defence in England and Wales, at the time of writing this book. You can find out what your local law is by contacting either the police or an organisation which gives advice to young people.

If you are attacked you have a legal right to defend yourself, using 'reasonable force', which means that it must be necessary at the time. The amount of force must be in relation to the degree of harm you are being threatened with. For example, it would clearly not be appropriate to shoot someone who only aimed to use very little force to grab your bag. If you have got rid of the attacker by using one technique, don't go on to injure them more. A court of law could be concerned about whether you avenged yourself or used too much force, rather than retreated from the attacker in self-defence. This is obviously a difficult judgement to make. As always, we do the best we can in each situation.

Weapons at hand can be used to defend yourself legally:

anything you would normally be carrying for your day-to-day studying or work, for instance keys, umbrellas or books. Don't carry a hammer around with you if you are not a carpenter or builder. However, it is illegal to carry any form of weapon, whether it is bought as a weapon or home-made (like a sharpened comb), just in case you are attacked. The police are allowed to stop and search you if they have reasonable suspicion that you are carrying any illegal item. It is up to you to prove that you didn't intend to use it illegally, but only for its normal purpose. Some items which have been in question in the past are keys, credit cards, coins and pocket knives. Items which you can carry for self-defence include personal alarms and umbrellas.

It is not possible to give information about the law in relation to every attack situation dealt with in this book. If you have any queries, contact your local police station, or some of the agencies listed in the following section.

Useful Contacts

The kind of organisation you may want to contact will depend on your particular experience and where you live. You may also find that the first agency you contact cannot offer the service you need, but it should be able to give you the telephone number of others that are more relevant. The organisations listed are only a sample selection of those which may be able to help you. For more information look in your local telephone directory or try a local information service.

England

A good starting point for information, suport and practical help is the many drop-in advice agencies around the country. In general they are easy to get hold of (by phone, or calling in), free, and experienced in the law. There are three main types of agency:

Youth Advice Agencies: these provide confidential initial support and some legal advice. They can be contacted through their national office:
The National Association of Young People's Counselling and Advisory Services (NAYPCAS)
17–23 Albion Street
Leicester LE1 6GD
Tel.: 0533 554775 Extensions 22 and 36
Some local authorities run general youth projects which can also offer support or refer people to other places, as can some local youth centres.

Law Centres: there are over fifty of these, mainly based in cities. They all offer free legal advice and representation, and will pass you on to a known outside solicitor if necessary.
The Law Centres Federation
Duchess House
18–19 Warren Street
London W1P 5DB
Tel.: 071 387 8570

Citizens Advice Bureaux: there are over 900 of these in England and Wales. The advice is free and confidential. CAB workers can give initial advice and support, explain the law, complete forms, or draft letters for you. They will also go to the police with you, or give you the name of a local solicitor.
National Association of Citizen's Advice Bureaux (NACAB)
Myddleton House
115–23 Pentonville Road
London N1 9LZ
Tel.: 071 833 2181

Other Sources of Help
Children's Legal Centre
20 Compton Terrace
London N1 2UN
Tel.: 071 359 6251
Advice concerning the law and young people's rights.
Open: Monday – Friday, 2–5 p.m.

Childline
Freepost 1111
London EC4B 4BB
Tel.: 0 800 1111
A free national 24-hour telephone helpline for young people in trouble or danger.

Rape Crisis Centre
PO Box 69
London WC1X 9NJ
Tel.: 071 837 1600/071 278 3956
There are rape crisis centres in most major cities. They offer support and counselling services to women of all ages who have been raped or sexually assaulted. Most of them provide support for young women experiencing incest.

Women and Girls Network
Box BCAM 8887
London WC1N 3XX
Tel.: 071 737 0577 (office)
      071 978 8887 (Helpline)

Self-defence Classes
You will need to phone around to find out what courses are available in your area. It will also depend on what you are looking for: self-defence or a martial arts (judo, aikido, etc.) classes.

You could contact your local town hall or youth service for details of courses. If, however, you can't find any information, contact the following organisation:

The London Self-defence Project
Women's Resource Centre
The Saga Centre
326 Kensal Road
London W10 5BZ
Tel.: 081 964 4656
      081 743 7827

Kaleghl Quinn Life Force
Arts Centre
2 West Heath Drive
London NW11 7QH
Tel.: 081 455 8698

Martial Arts Commission
Broadway House
15/16 Deptford Broadway
London SE8 4PE
Tel.: 081 691 3433

Wales

Cardiff Rape Crisis
c/o Women's Centre
2 Coburn Street
Cathays
Cardiff
Tel.: 0222 484222
Provide support, counselling and information

Rape Crisis Line and Incest Survivors Service
Abbey Road Centre
9 Abbey Road
Bangor
Gwynedd
LL57 2EA
Tel.: 0248 354885

Scotland

Dundee Rape Crisis
PO Box 83
Dundee
Tel.: 0382 201291

Edinburgh Rape Crisis Centre
PO Box 120
Head Post Office
Brunwick Road
Edinburgh
EH1 3ND
Tel.: 041 221 8448

Women's Support Project
Newlands Centre
871 Springfield Road
Glasgow
G31 4HQ
Tel.: 041 554 5669
Information, resources and support for adult and young women

Highland Rape Crisis and Counselling Centre
PO Box 58
Inverness
Highland
Tel.: 0349 65316

Northern Ireland

Belfast Rape Crisis Centre
PO Box 46
Belfast
BT2 7AR
Tel.: 0232 249696

Eire

Dublin Rape Crisis Centre
70 Lower Lesson Street
Dublin 2
Tel.: 068 614911/613923/614561

Cork Rape Crisis Centre
27a McCurtain Street
Cork
Tel.: 021 968086

Australia

Northern Territory
Office of Women's Affairs
Tel.: (089) 896304

Queensland
Women's Information Service
Tel.: (07) 229 1580

Victoria
Women's Information and Referral Exchange
Tel.: (03) 654 6844

New South Wales
Women's Health Advisory Service
Tel.: (02) 331 5014

Western Australia
Women's Information and Referral Exchange
Tel.: (09) 222 0444

New Zealand

There are a variety of organisations which give support to women of all ages in New Zealand. We have provided details of those based in major cities. Contact them for details of others in either the South or North Island.

Help Foundation Auckland
PO Box 68–152, Newton
Auckland
Tel.: (09) 399–185/(09) 389–622

Rape Crisis
PO Box 5424
Dunedin
Tel.: (024) 741–592

Te Kahano O Te Whanau Ki Tamaki
PO Box 8405
Symonds Street
Auckland
Tel.: (09) 302–1604

Te Puna Oranga
PO Box 13460
Armagh Street
Christchurch
Tel.: (03) 655–715

Self-defence Classes
There is a national Maori organisation which offers self-defence classes through a network of teachers. Contact them for details of classes in or near your area:

Whakamaru Tinana
PO Box 21260
Edgeware
Christchurch
Tel.: (03) 557–780/(03) 483–595.

USA

Los Angeles Commission on Assaults Against Women
543 North Fairfax
Los Angeles
California 90036
Tel.: 213 655 4235
Self-defence classes for adult and young women

Santa Cruz City Commission for the Prevention of Violence
Against Women
City Hall
809 Centre Street
Santa Cruz
California 95060
Tel.: 408 429 3546
Provide self-defence classes, information and advice

Child Abuse Prevention Project (CAPP)
PO Box 2005
Columbus
Ohio 43202
Tel.: 614 291 2540
Prevention and support service for young women

Safety and Fitness Exchange (SAFE) inc
541 Sixth Avenue
New York
NY 10011
Tel.: 212 242 4874
Supportive classes in realistic self-defence for adult and young
women

Canada

Kids Help Phoneline
(National free phone)
Tel.: 1 800 668 6868

Sexual Assault Centre
388 Dundas Street
London
Ontario
N6B 1V7
Tel.: 519 438 2272
24 hours Answering Service for those who have been sexually
assaulted

Coalition of Rape Crisis Centres
PO Box 1929
302 King Street
Peterborough
Ontario K9J 7X7

Self-defence classes
Many self-defence classes are held locally. Ring your local
Parks and Recreation Office or your local YWCA, who should
be able to provide you with details of these. If they cannot
give the information you are looking for, contact one of the
following:

Wen-Do Women's Self-Defence
2 Carlton Street
Suite 817
Toronto
Ontario M5B IJ3
Tel.: 416 533 1202

Women Educating in Self-Defence Training
2349 St. Catherine's Street
Vancouver
British Columbia
V5T 3X8
Tel.: 604 876 6390

Self-Defence for Women and Children
60 Rang 11, RR 4
Arthabaska
Quebec G6P 6S1
Tel.: 819 357 8868

Other Virago Upstarts

OUT IN THE OPEN
A Guide for Young People Who Have Been Sexually Abused

Ouainé Bain and Maureen Sanders

'The most surprising thing for me was to find out that it wasn't some weird thing that happened just to me'

If you have ever experienced any kind of sexual abuse, this book is for you. Plain-speaking and sympathetic, it cuts through the terrible loneliness and silence and talks frankly about the range of feelings sexually abused young people experience. Including other people's stories and discussing honestly what can happen once the truth is told, it also offers practical advice and encouragement to young people on the road to recovery. Ultimately this is an optimistic book, arguing and believing that despite the pain, anger, fears and setbacks, once things are out in the open, victims *can* become survivors.

LOVE TALK
A Young Person's Guide To Sex, Love and Life

Eleanor Stephens

With Cartoons by Jonathan Bairstow

A Channel Four Book to tie in with a ten-part TV series

Sex, love and all that stuff can be fun, exciting, enthralling and, for teenagers, a mine-field. Firmly believing that once they have information that is accurate and accessible, young people are capable of handling the powerful changes and important choices that characterise this period, Eleanor Stephens and Jonathan Bairstow have produced an invaluable book to help young people in life and love.

Contents:
Body Talk • Mind Talk • Sex Talk • The First Time
Safe Loving • Birth Control • Who Am I? • Coping With
Love • How Do I Look? • Baby Talk • Health Check
Sex-Related Diseases • Sex And The Law • Jealousy
• Friendship

THE YOUNG PERSON'S GUIDE TO SAVING THE PLANET

Debbie Silver and Bernadette Vallely

All you ever wanted to know about the environment but didn't know who to ask, where to look, what to do . . .

Acid rain, batteries, beauty, CFCs, deodorants, E numbers, the greenhouse effect, hamburgers, noise, the ozone layer, rainforests, television, whales . . . over one hundred environmental issues are all here in a simple A–Z format. But that's only the beginning. This book shows you what action *you* can take, ranging from small life changes to ways of encouraging family, friends, schools, supermarkets – even industry and governments – to 'go green'. Saving the planet is a tall order. But it's our only world and our only chance. You could make a difference.

THE YOUNG PERSON'S GUIDE TO ANIMAL RIGHTS

Barbara James

Following the great success of *The Young Person's Guide to Saving the Planet*, *The Young Person's Guide to Animal Rights* is concerned with an equally urgent issue. How do we know where to draw the line if we care about animals? Do we refuse veal, but eat beef? Become vegetarian, but wear leather? In order to make up our minds about what we really think, we must know the facts. In the A–Z format, up-to-date information and statistics are given on over 100 related topics such as beauty without cruelty, dissection, dog-fighting, circuses and warfare. This invaluable easy-to-use guide tells us all we need to know, and in each section answers the important question: 'What can you do?'

VOICES FROM HOME
Girls Talk About Their Families

Sue Sharpe

'When I'm older I can be nicer to my parents and do things without having to lie' – Lai

'I remember my dad saying, "Get out of this house, you upset your mum and me so much"' – Ellie

'I always know they'll stick up for me, whatever. It's something I can't describe, the bond in my family' – Gwyn

Voices From Home explodes the myth of the cosy, happy family into a kaleidoscope of changing patterns. Girls describe their life at home – haven or hell, or both. Here closeness and security jostle with violence and abuse. These are real families – some together, some apart – and no matter what shape it takes, for most girls, family life still pivots around a powerful sense of love and loyalty.

SPEAKING OUT
Black Girls in Britain

Audrey Osler

'I want my future here in Britain. I consider it to be my country' – Mumtaz

'My ambition, my one great ambition, is to make it known that Black people can get somewhere' – Gillian

'I hope that white people will read this. They'll find out what Asian and Afro-Caribbean girls think and get a trace of what our lives are like' – Nazrah

Teachers and school; friends and boyfriends; parents and families; the community and the wider world all come under lively and passionate scrutiny in this book. Though painfully, angrily aware of racism and sexism, these girls have an optimistic eye for the future and thought-provoking ideas for change now. Surprising, sobering, revealing – nothing is sacred in *Speaking Out*.

TRANSFORMING MOMENTS

Edited by Scarlett MccGwire

'Revelation! It wasn't like a religious experience or anything, significant moments never are. It's that slow dawning of recognition . . .'

Maya Angelou, Melanie McFadyean, Priscilla Presley, Diane Abbott, Eileen Fairweather and Shreela Ghosh, among others, look to their teenage years to find a turning point that altered the course of their lives. What an extraordinary range of stories emerge: first love in a Jewish ghetto; betrayal and expulsion from school; the exhilaration of leaving home; the impact of Jimi Hendrix; teetering on the brink of suicide; refusing to believe the teacher who says university is not for the likes of you. In all our lives are moments or events – dramatic or quiet – that leave us with the certainty that never again will we be quite the same . . .

FALLING FOR LOVE
Teenage Mothers Talk

Sue Sharpe

'To start with I felt ashamed of myself really. But after he was born I thought, why should I care what anybody else thinks? It's great to have a baby'.

Becoming a mother when you're still a teenager means growing up fast, with not much freedom and a lot of responsibility. But it can add an enormous amount of love and meaning to life. In *Falling for Love*, young mothers give their own stories – telling how boyfriends and parents, schoolfriends and teachers have reacted. They also talk about adoption, living with parents or alone, coping with school or work, and the joys and troubles of having a child when you're still very young. It can happen to anyone, and this sensitive and moving book tells what it's really like.